Greetings, beavers!

MARVELS ANIMALS 17

BEAVERS

QUINN M. ARNOLD

CREATIVE EDUCATION | CREATIVE PAPERBACKS

table of contents

Greetings, Beavers! 1
Busy Builders. 7
Beaver Tails 8
Teeth for Trees. 10
Time to Eat! 12
Beaver Kits 14
What Do Beavers Do? 16
Farewell, Beavers! 18
Picture a Beaver 20
Words to Know 22
Read More 22
Websites 22
Index. 24

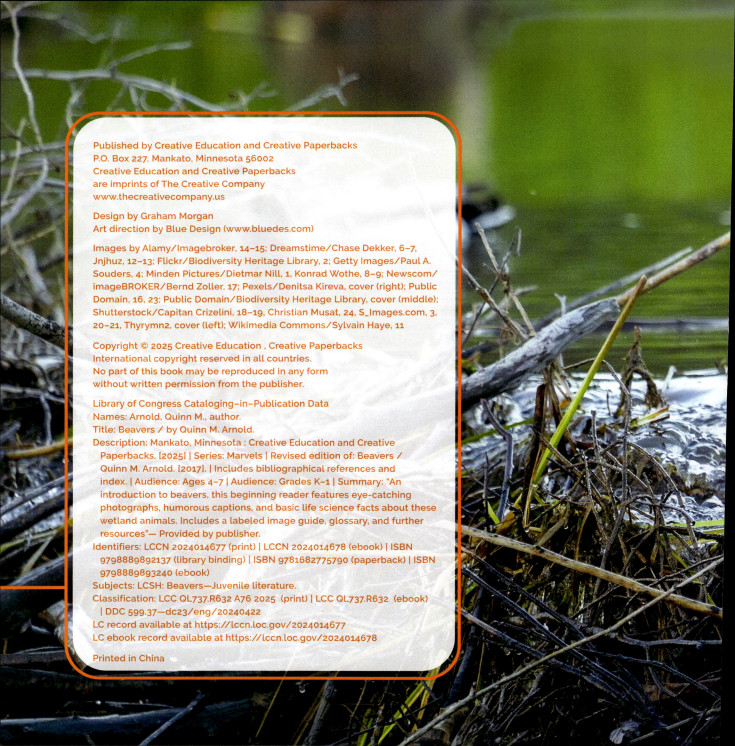

Published by Creative Education and Creative Paperbacks
P.O. Box 227, Mankato, Minnesota 56002
Creative Education and Creative Paperbacks
are imprints of The Creative Company
www.thecreativecompany.us

Design by Graham Morgan
Art direction by Blue Design (www.bluedes.com)

Images by Alamy/Imagebroker, 14–15; Dreamstime/Chase Dekker, 6–7, Jnjhuz, 12–13; Flickr/Biodiversity Heritage Library, 2; Getty Images/Paul A. Souders, 4; Minden Pictures/Dietmar Nill, 1, Konrad Wothe, 8–9; Newscom/imageBROKER/Bernd Zoller, 17; Pexels/Denitsa Kireva, cover (right); Public Domain, 16, 23; Public Domain/Biodiversity Heritage Library, cover (middle); Shutterstock/Capitan Crizelini, 18–19, Christian Musat, 24, S_Images.com, 3, 20–21, Thyrymn2, cover (left); Wikimedia Commons/Sylvain Haye, 11

Copyright © 2025 Creative Education , Creative Paperbacks
International copyright reserved in all countries.
No part of this book may be reproduced in any form
without written permission from the publisher.

Library of Congress Cataloging-in-Publication Data
Names: Arnold, Quinn M., author.
Title: Beavers / by Quinn M. Arnold.
Description: Mankato, Minnesota : Creative Education and Creative Paperbacks, [2025] | Series: Marvels | Revised edition of: Beavers / Quinn M. Arnold. [2017]. | Includes bibliographical references and index. | Audience: Ages 4–7 | Audience: Grades K–1 | Summary: "An introduction to beavers, this beginning reader features eye-catching photographs, humorous captions, and basic life science facts about these wetland animals. Includes a labeled image guide, glossary, and further resources"— Provided by publisher.
Identifiers: LCCN 2024014677 (print) | LCCN 2024014678 (ebook) | ISBN 9798889892137 (library binding) | ISBN 9781682775790 (paperback) | ISBN 9798889893240 (ebook)
Subjects: LCSH: Beavers—Juvenile literature.
Classification: LCC QL737.R632 A76 2025 (print) | LCC QL737.R632 (ebook) | DDC 599.37—dc23/eng/20240422
LC record available at https://lccn.loc.gov/2024014677
LC ebook record available at https://lccn.loc.gov/2024014678

Printed in China

Beavers live in wooded places. They build **dams** in water. A pond forms behind the dam. Beavers build a home there.

Beaver fur can be brown or black. The tail is big and flat. A beaver's back feet are **webbed**. This helps it swim.

Beavers have big front teeth. They are orange and sharp.

Beavers chew through trees. They use the trees in the dam.

A BEAVER'S TEETH ARE ALWAYS GROWING.

Hungry beavers eat wood and tree bark. They eat plants, too. Beavers store food for winter.

BEAVER KITS CAN SWIM WHEN THEY ARE FOUR DAYS OLD.

Kits are baby beavers. They drink milk from their mother. Kits stay with their family about two years.

Busy beavers work on their dams. They gather food at night. They dive underwater.

[Picture a Beaver]

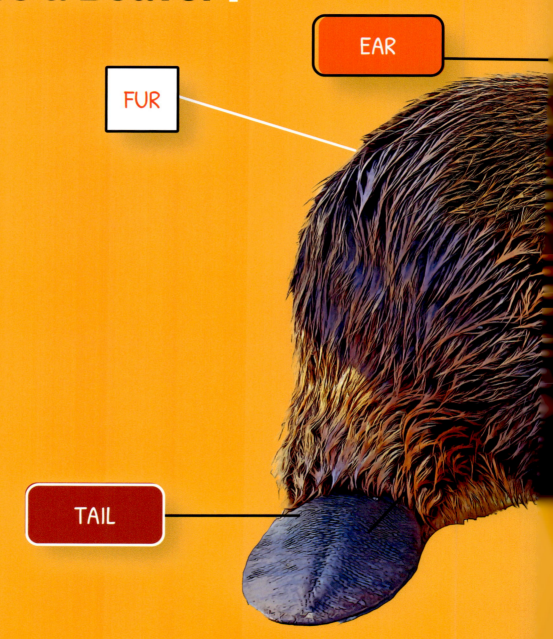

EAR

FUR

20

TAIL

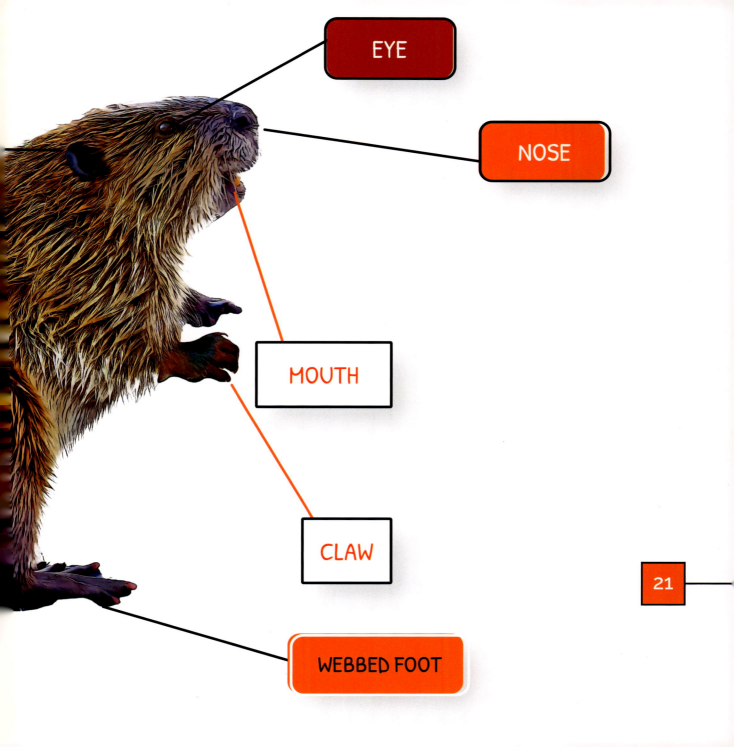

WORDS TO KNOW

dam: a barrier across a river or stream made of trees, branches, and other natural materials

bark: the tough outer covering of a woody plant

webbed: connected with skin

READ MORE

Perdew, Laura. *Beaver Colonies*. Mendota Heights, Minn.: Focus Readers, 2025.

Schwartz, Heather E. *Meet a Baby Beaver*. Minneapolis: Lerner Publications, 2024.

WEBSITES

8 Facts to Celebrate International Beaver Day
https://nationalzoo.si.edu/animals/news/8-facts-celebrate-international-beaver-day
Get the scoop about these big rodents with big teeth.

Beavers
https://kids.nationalgeographic.com/animals/mammals/facts/beaver
Find more fun facts about beavers in North America.

INDEX

dams, 7, 10, 16
feet, 9, 21
food, 12, 15, 16
fur, 9, 20
kits, 14, 15
ponds, 7
swimming, 9, 16
tails, 9, 20
teeth, 10, 11